IMPRESSIONS · OF

Kerry

Ph

D1476430

Li

Introduction by **T. J. Barrington**

e Press

First published and printed by the
Appletree Press Ltd, 7 James
Street South, Belfast BT2 8DL.
Photographs © Liam Blake, 1986.
Text © T. J. Barrington, 1986. All
rights reserved.

First published in Britain 1987

British Library Cataloguing in
Publication Data
Blake, Liam
    Impressions of Kerry.
    1. Kerry (Ireland) —
    Description and Travel
    I. Title
    914.19'604824   DA990.K4

ISBN 0-86281-182-1

9 8 7 6 5 4 3 2 1

Introduction

WHEN I was a child I wasted much salt trying to catch birds by putting it on their tails. I am at a like task in trying to capture the personality of Kerry in words. The place itself is protean; the weather marvellously inconstant; and the people draw shape and colour from the interactions of place and weather, adding, of course, their own dashes of change and complexity. To put it too simply, there are three main elements in the personality of Kerry — the places, the weather and the people, each highly mobile and all contributing much complexity. After all, 'personality' comes from the mask, the *persona,* behind which the ancient Greek actor portrayed now this character, now that.

Let me try to explain. One misty day I spent time at Aghadoe overlooking the Lower Lake of Killarney, a scene I knew well — the line of Cork mountains, the spent volcanoes, the mountains backing Killarney itself, Mangerton with its great corrie and Torc, and

3

the toothed Macgillycuddy Reeks. There was the shapely spire of Pugin's cathedral, and the bright semi-circle cast by Brickeen Bridge over the link between the Middle and Lower Lakes; branching from the former the twist in the Killarney Valley that contains the exquisite Upper Lake; in the foreground the Lower Lake with its many islands. In all, one of the world's great views.

But, this day, the view had its own ideas about revealing itself — now with dazzling clarity, now as if grudgingly, now totally shut off. Now the towering mountains, now only the nearer islands, now just nothing. Exasperating, thrilling — and insightful. If so great a stretch of landscape could become so insubstantial, how real was reality? I was reminded of the Greek philosopher with his saying that 'That which is is not greater than that which is not.' This mobility of landscape — this mountain that now is there and now is not — is a feature not only of Killarney but of much of Kerry, especially of the great peninsulas and the mist-prone seascapes, a mobility of reality that is a major influence on the interplay of those who live in such contingent places.

That was some twenty years ago. The other part of that insight dates from twenty years earlier when I went to the greyhound track in Tralee with two prominent Tralee men, one a breeder of greyhounds.

Come the first race, and the breeder asked his friend to find out the owner of a dog he had picked out, my race card being contemptuously brushed aside. Back came the friend, there were some whispers, and the breeder told me that the dog would win; which it did. It was the same with each race. At the end of seven races the breeder had picked six clear winners and one partner in a dead heat. When I congratulated him on his marvellous eye for a dog, he smiled pityingly at my innocence. Forty years ago in Kerry greyhound racing was in a state of nature and none of the formal information about the dogs could be relied upon — owner, form, breeding, colour, or the rest. The only thing that could not be disguised was the excitement of the young handler as before the race he led around the dog that would win. That was the chink on which my friend based his unerring judgement. It was a lesson on how to cope with that which is being just a bit greater than that which is not!

This interplay of shadow and substance is seen as a fencing match with wit, verbal or situational, for rapier. 'That,' as an old friend said, 'is the fun of it for us in Kerry.' Many of the stories of Daniel O'Connell's successes in the Kerry courts depended on his grasp of the rules of this game, its taboos and its opportunities. The verbal part of it comes from a long Gaelic tradition of giving high value to the ready-tongued. O'Connell's grandmother was a famous practitioner of rhymed repartee in Irish. To this day the rhymed retorts of the Great Dan's 'court poet', Tomas Rua O Suilleabhain, are quoted and savoured. In the Gaeltacht areas, for example west of Dingle, there survives in Irish this delight in verbal dexterity and wit. All of this is carried on in, to the outsider, a fascinating ambience of charm and personal warmth. This skill has been carried into English. On a farm high above Kilmakilloge south-west of Kenmare I was seeking out one of the stone circles special to that area, being shown the way by a charming old farmer. As we climbed up he said, 'You'd be an Englishman, now, wouldn't you?' Although I was accustomed to the implication that only an Englishman would be interested in our heritage, I answered rather crossly, 'No! I'm a Dublin man.' 'English?' he replied gently. 'Ah, I thought not.'

There is a deep-rooted pride in the county and its people, sometimes, as in relation to its astonishing prowess on the football field, unassailably based; sometimes, as in the title 'The Kingdom' (deriving as it does from a crude eighteenth-century mistranslation) giving a shaky sense of separateness. How often does one hear, as if to buttress this, 'Well, we like to do things our own way in Kerry.' But sometimes pride rests on fantasy, as when, during

World War II, an old friend asked me to explain the policy on neutrality. When I came to the conditional bit — 'If the British attack us we join the Germans; if the Germans attack we join the British' — he stopped me. 'Join the British,' he exclaimed. 'That would never be accepted in Kerry.' 'What choice would you have?' I asked. 'Easy,' he said. 'We'd close the frontier at Rathmore and proclaim our neutrality.' Or the famous remark of the old lady in Tralee when the coinage was being decimalised: 'Sure, 'twill never catch on in Kerry.'

This is not to say that facts are ignored. Many stories illustrate the preternatural capacity of the citizens of Cahersiveen to divine what is going on. My favourite is that of the German spy in World War II, landed nearby, instructed to go to a pub in the town, meet (let us say) Mick O'Shea, and give him the password 'Carrantoohil will be white with snow this night.' In the pub there was, apart from the publican, no one. After a couple of pints the German inquired, 'Is there a Mick O'Shea around here?' 'Good God,' said the publican, 'the place is full of them. We have Mick the Post, Mick the Boat, Mick the Smith —dozens. Indeed, I'm Mick O'Shea myself.' 'Ah,' said the German, 'Carrantoohil will be white with snow this night.' 'I have you now!' exclaimed the publican. 'The man you want is Mick the Spy.'

But let us come back to the rapier, the dexterous

meiosis. We once rented a house beautifully situated close to the arc of the mountains above Sneem. Close by was a place called Glorach, meaning noisy, from the terrifying mountain winds that howled and bellowed through it. A Sneem woman asked me where we were staying. When I told her, she said thoughtfully with that rising intonation that puts one on the alert, 'Ah, yes. A fine airy place.' Of all the pleasures of Kerry I think this is the one I most enjoy, the mastery of ambiguity laced with charm, the culture fine tuned to put you down ever so gently.

There is, of course, culture in a more formal sense — from the tip of Dingle peninsula some one hundred books in Irish in this century, one of them a masterpiece; the concentration of literary talent in English in and around Listowel, with its annual Writers' Week (when a giant tanker got stuck in one of the narow streets a passer-by commented, 'Ink for Writers' Week'); the concentration of traditional music around Sliabh Luachra between Killarney and Castleisland; the unique and charming Siamsa Tire centred on Tralee; and much more. And everywhere the talk, the wit, the stories and, above all, the delight in the nice use of words to explore the reaches of fun and fantasy.

So it is easy to love not only the beautiful places but also the marvellously sophisticated people and the culture the interaction of place and people has produced. I hope Liam Blake's visual portrayal of the reality of place will lead many more to these farther shores.

T. J. BARRINGTON

Gallarus Oratory

Dawn over Dingle peninsula
from Mount Eagle ➤

◄ Horses near Killarney

Connor Pass ►

16

◄On Great Skellig

Dunbeg Fort, near
Slea Head

Minard Castle, Dingle

◄Ring of Kerry from Dingle peninsula

◄ Dingle harbour in fog

Pub door, Dingle ►

Kilmacader, Dingle peninsula

Gallarus Oratory

Winter snow on Macgillycuddy's Reeks ➤

◄On Valentia Island

Collecting turf near Brandon Creek

Looking toward the Connor Pass ►

◄ Inishtooskert, Blasket Islands

After the storm, Ballinskelligs ►

◄ Inishtooskert from Slea Head

Waterlilies, Gap of Dunloe ►

◄Gap of Dunloe

From the Healy Pass

◄ Torc waterfall

Dunes, Inch Strand ►

Coumeenole Strand,
Dingle peninsula

Farmhouse, Black Valley ➤

◄ Staigue Fort, near Castlecove

O'Shea's Bar, Sneem

◀In Dingle town

◄ Clogher Head, Dingle peninsula

Great Blasket and Tearaght from Dunquin ►